It is a wet day.
Colin, the big cat, is wet in his bin.

He gets up. He goes to see Wellington in the kennel.

'I am wet,' says Colin.
'Can I come in the kennel with you?'

'No,' says Wellington.
'The kennel is full.
You cannot come in.'

Colin is sad. He goes to see the hen. 'Can I come in?' he says.

'No,' says the hen. 'The hut is full. You cannot come in.'

Colin is sad. He goes to see Jelly in the shed.

'You are wet,' says Jelly. 'Come in.'
Colin is happy.